WILLIAM SHAKESPEARE
Diary 2015

I0477046

PERSONAL INFORMATION

NAME	
ADDRESS	
E-MAIL	
PHONE	
MOBILE	

DIARY 2015

PERSONAL INFORMATION

NAME	
ADDRESS	
E-MAIL	
PHONE	
MOBILE	

2 0 1 5

January

Su	Mo	Tu	We	Th	Fr	Sa
				1	2	3
4	5	6	7	8	9	10
11	12	13	14	15	16	17
18	19	20	21	22	23	24
25	26	27	28	29	30	31

February

Su	Mo	Tu	We	Th	Fr	Sa
1	2	3	4	5	6	7
8	9	10	11	12	13	14
15	16	17	18	19	20	21
22	23	24	25	26	27	28

March

Su	Mo	Tu	We	Th	Fr	Sa
1	2	3	4	5	6	7
8	9	10	11	12	13	14
15	16	17	18	19	20	21
22	23	24	25	26	27	28
29	30	31				

April

Su	Mo	Tu	We	Th	Fr	Sa
			1	2	3	4
5	6	7	8	9	10	11
12	13	14	15	16	17	18
19	20	21	22	23	24	25
26	27	28	29	30		

May

Su	Mo	Tu	We	Th	Fr	Sa
31					1	2
3	4	5	6	7	8	9
10	11	12	13	14	15	16
17	18	19	20	21	22	23
24	25	26	27	28	29	30

June

Su	Mo	Tu	We	Th	Fr	Sa
	1	2	3	4	5	6
7	8	9	10	11	12	13
14	15	16	17	18	19	20
21	22	23	24	25	26	27
28	29	30				

July

Su	Mo	Tu	We	Th	Fr	Sa
			1	2	3	4
5	6	7	8	9	10	11
12	13	14	15	16	17	18
19	20	21	22	23	24	25
26	27	28	29	30	31	

August

Su	Mo	Tu	We	Th	Fr	Sa
30	31					1
2	3	4	5	6	7	8
9	10	11	12	13	14	15
16	17	18	19	20	21	22
23	24	25	26	27	28	29

September

Su	Mo	Tu	We	Th	Fr	Sa
		1	2	3	4	5
6	7	8	9	10	11	12
13	14	15	16	17	18	19
20	21	22	23	24	25	26
27	28	29	30			

October

Su	Mo	Tu	We	Th	Fr	Sa
				1	2	3
4	5	6	7	8	9	10
11	12	13	14	15	16	17
18	19	20	21	22	23	24
25	26	27	28	29	30	31

November

Su	Mo	Tu	We	Th	Fr	Sa
1	2	3	4	5	6	7
8	9	10	11	12	13	14
15	16	17	18	19	20	21
22	23	24	25	26	27	28
29	30					

December

Su	Mo	Tu	We	Th	Fr	Sa
		1	2	3	4	5
6	7	8	9	10	11	12
13	14	15	16	17	18	19
20	21	22	23	24	25	26
27	28	29	30	31		

2016

January

Su	Mo	Tu	We	Th	Fr	Sa
					1	2
3	4	5	6	7	8	9
10	11	12	13	14	15	16
17	18	19	20	21	22	23
24	25	26	27	28	29	30
31						

February

Su	Mo	Tu	We	Th	Fr	Sa
	1	2	3	4	5	6
7	8	9	10	11	12	13
14	15	16	17	18	19	20
21	22	23	24	25	26	27
28	29					

March

Su	Mo	Tu	We	Th	Fr	Sa
		1	2	3	4	5
6	7	8	9	10	11	12
13	14	15	16	17	18	19
20	21	22	23	24	25	26
27	28	29	30	31		

April

Su	Mo	Tu	We	Th	Fr	Sa
					1	2
3	4	5	6	7	8	9
10	11	12	13	14	15	16
17	18	19	20	21	22	23
24	25	26	27	28	29	30

May

Su	Mo	Tu	We	Th	Fr	Sa
1	2	3	4	5	6	7
8	9	10	11	12	13	14
15	16	17	18	19	20	21
22	23	24	25	26	27	28
29	30	31				

June

Su	Mo	Tu	We	Th	Fr	Sa
			1	2	3	4
5	6	7	8	9	10	11
12	13	14	15	16	17	18
19	20	21	22	23	24	25
26	27	28	29	30		

July

Su	Mo	Tu	We	Th	Fr	Sa
					1	2
3	4	5	6	7	8	9
10	11	12	13	14	15	16
17	18	19	20	21	22	23
24	25	26	27	28	29	30
31						

August

Su	Mo	Tu	We	Th	Fr	Sa
	1	2	3	4	5	6
7	8	9	10	11	12	13
14	15	16	17	18	19	20
21	22	23	24	25	26	27
28	29	30	31			

September

Su	Mo	Tu	We	Th	Fr	Sa
				1	2	3
4	5	6	7	8	9	10
11	12	13	14	15	16	17
18	19	20	21	22	23	24
25	26	27	28	29	30	

October

Su	Mo	Tu	We	Th	Fr	Sa
						1
2	3	4	5	6	7	8
9	10	11	12	13	14	15
16	17	18	19	20	21	22
23	24	25	26	27	28	29
30	31					

November

Su	Mo	Tu	We	Th	Fr	Sa
		1	2	3	4	5
6	7	8	9	10	11	12
13	14	15	16	17	18	19
20	21	22	23	24	25	26
27	28	29	30			

December

Su	Mo	Tu	We	Th	Fr	Sa
				1	2	3
4	5	6	7	8	9	10
11	12	13	14	15	16	17
18	19	20	21	22	23	24
25	26	27	28	29	30	31

New Year's Day
Thursday
1

Friday
2

Saturday
3

Sunday
4

Monday

5

Tuesday

6

Wednesday

7

Thursday
8

Friday
9

Saturday
10

Sunday
11

Monday
12

Tuesday
13

Wednesday
14

Thursday
15

Friday
16

Saturday
17

Sunday
18

Monday
19

Tuesday
20

Wednesday
21

Thursday
22

Friday
23

Saturday
24

Sunday
25

Monday
26

Tuesday
27

Wednesday
28

Thursday
29

Friday
30

Saturday
31

Sunday
1

Monday

2

Tuesday

3

Wednesday

4

Thursday
5

Friday
6

Saturday
7

Sunday
8

February 2015

Monday
9

Tuesday
10

Wednesday
11

Thursday
12

Friday
13

Saturday
14

Sunday
15

February 2015

Monday
16

Tuesday
17

Wednesday
18

Thursday
19

Friday
20

Saturday
21

Sunday
22

February 2015

Monday
23

Tuesday
24

Wednesday
25

Thursday
26

Friday
27

Saturday
28

Sunday
1

Monday

2

Tuesday

3

Wednesday

4

Thursday
5

Friday
6

Saturday
7

Sunday
8

March 2015

Monday
9

Tuesday
10

Wednesday
11

Thursday
12

Friday
13

Saturday
14

Sunday
15

Monday

16

Tuesday

17

Wednesday

18

Thursday
19

Friday
20

Saturday
21

Sunday
22

March 2015

Monday
23

Tuesday
24

Wednesday
25

Thursday
26

Friday
27

Saturday
28

Sunday
29

Monday
30

Tuesday
31

Wednesday
1

Thursday
2

Good Friday

Friday
3

Saturday
4

Easter Sunday

Sunday
5

April 2015

Monday
Monday

6

Tuesday

7

Wednesday

8

Thursday
9

Friday
10

Saturday
11

Sunday
12

Monday
13

Tuesday
14

Wednesday
15

Thursday
16

Friday
17

Saturday
18

Sunday
19

Monday
20

Tuesday
21

Wednesday
22

Thursday
23

Friday
24

Saturday
25

Sunday
26

April 2015

Monday
27

Tuesday
28

Wednesday
29

Thursday
30

Friday
1

Saturday
2

Sunday
3

Monday
Holiday

Early May Bank

4

Tuesday

5

Wednesday

6

Thursday
7

Friday
8

Saturday
9

Sunday
10

Monday
11

Tuesday
12

Wednesday
13

Thursday
14

Friday
15

Saturday
16

Sunday
17

Monday
18

Tuesday
19

Wednesday
20

Thursday
21

Friday
22

Saturday
23

Sunday
24

Monday
Holiday
25

Spring Bank

Tuesday
26

Wednesday
27

Thursday
28

Friday
29

Saturday
30

Sunday
31

June 2015

Monday
1

Tuesday
2

Wednesday
3

Thursday
4

Friday
5

Saturday
6

Sunday
7

Monday

8

Tuesday

9

Wednesday

10

Thursday
11

Friday
12

Saturday
13

Sunday
14

Monday
15

Tuesday
16

Wednesday
17

Thursday
18

Friday
19

Saturday
20

Sunday
21

Monday
22

Tuesday
23

Wednesday
24

Thursday
25

Friday
26

Saturday
27

Sunday
28

Monday
29

Tuesday
30

Wednesday
1

Thursday
2

Friday
3

Saturday
4

Sunday
5

Monday

6

Tuesday

7

Wednesday

8

Thursday
9

Friday
10

Saturday
11

Sunday
12

Monday
13

Tuesday
14

Wednesday
15

Thursday
16

Friday
17

Saturday
18

Sunday
19

July 2015

Monday
20

Tuesday
21

Wednesday
22

Thursday
23

Friday
24

Saturday
25

Sunday
26

Monday
27

Tuesday
28

Wednesday
29

Thursday
30

Friday
31

Saturday
1

Sunday
2

Monday

3

Tuesday

4

Wednesday

5

Thursday
6

Friday
7

Saturday
8

Sunday
9

Monday
10

Tuesday
11

Wednesday
12

Thursday
13

Friday
14

Saturday
15

Sunday
16

Monday
17

Tuesday
18

Wednesday
19

Thursday
20

Friday
21

Saturday
22

Sunday
23

Monday
24

Tuesday
25

Wednesday
26

Thursday
27

Friday
28

Saturday
29

Sunday
30

Monday

Holiday

Summer Bank

31

Tuesday

1

Wednesday

2

Thursday
3

Friday
4

Saturday
5

Sunday
6

September 2015

Monday

7

Tuesday

8

Wednesday

9

Thursday
10

Friday
11

Saturday
12

Sunday
13

Monday
14

Tuesday
15

Wednesday
16

Thursday
17

Friday
18

Saturday
19

Sunday
20

September 2015

Monday
21

Tuesday
22

Wednesday
23

80

Thursday
24

Friday
25

Saturday
26

Sunday
27

Monday
28

Tuesday
29

Wednesday
30

Thursday

1

Friday

2

Saturday

3

Sunday

4

Monday

5

Tuesday

6

Wednesday

7

Thursday
8

Friday
9

Saturday
10

Sunday
11

Monday

12

Tuesday

13

Wednesday

14

Thursday
15

Friday
16

Saturday
17

Sunday
18

Monday
19

Tuesday
20

Wednesday
21

Thursday
22

Friday
23

Saturday
24

Sunday
25

Monday
26

Tuesday
27

Wednesday
28

Thursday
29

Friday
30

Saturday
31

Sunday
1

November 2015

Monday

2

Tuesday

3

Wednesday

4

Thursday
5

Friday
6

Saturday
7

Sunday
8

Monday

9

Tuesday

10

Wednesday

11

Thursday
12

Friday
13

Saturday
14

Sunday
15

Monday
16

Tuesday
17

Wednesday
18

Thursday
19

Friday
20

Saturday
21

Sunday
22

Monday
23

Tuesday
24

Wednesday
25

Thursday
26

Friday
27

Saturday
28

Sunday
29

Monday

30

Tuesday

1

Wednesday

2

Thursday

3

Friday

4

Saturday

5

Sunday

6

Monday

7

Tuesday

8

Wednesday

9

Thursday
10

Friday
11

Saturday
12

Sunday
13

Monday

14

Tuesday

15

Wednesday

16

Thursday
17

Friday
18

Saturday
19

Sunday
20

December 2015

Monday
21

Tuesday
22

Wednesday
23

Thursday
24

Christmas Day
Friday
25

Saturday
26

Sunday
27

December 2015

Monday **28**	Boxing Day Holiday

Tuesday
29

Wednesday
30

Thursday
31

New Year's Day
Friday
1

Saturday
2

Sunday
3

Monday
4

Tuesday
5

Wednesday
6

MY CONTACTS

NAME	MOBILE	EMAIL
